Canada

CANADA

Photography and text by

Edmund Nägele F.R.P.S.

Produced by

Ted Smart & David Gibbon

Colour Library International

Introduction

Canada is vast – far larger than any other member of the Commonwealth – and the second largest country in the world. It stretches from the Atlantic Ocean to the Pacific Ocean and from the United States border to the North Pole. Halifax on the east coast is farther from Vancouver on the west coast than it is from London. Such staggering vastness is a dominating feature because it creates a diversity of climate and vegetation that has greatly influenced the human environment and also because much is a huge area that is still undeveloped and, indeed, at present is still undevelopable.

Archaeologists have established the existence of an Indian culture in Newfoundland more than 4,000 years ago. Excavation has disclosed that adventurous Vikings visited and lived there around 1000 A.D. Recorded history credits John Cabot, sailing from Bristol in 1497, as being the first European to reach Newfoundland. Further voyages in the 16th and 17th centuries were attempts to find a North-West Passage through to Asia. Land expeditions were even more difficult in such unhospitable terrain. Cartier discovered the St. Lawrence river and claimed the land for the King of France in 1534. French interest continued and Champlain founded settlements in Nova Scotia and Quebec. In spite of hostile Indians and severe climate New France became a reality when trading posts were established. Other countries became interested and the Hudson's Bay Company was founded by the English in 1670 and speedily rivalled the French with their settlements and fur trading. The climax came in 1759 when General Wolfe stormed Quebec and General Montcalm capitulated. Canada came under British rule, but the French were allowed to keep their lands, language, religion and laws. After the American War of Independence many colonists preferred to remain under British rule and moved north into Canada.

British emigrants arrived in increasing numbers and it was decided to divide the country into Upper, or British, Canada and Lower, or French, Canada. In 1840 the Act of Union made Canada one nation and in 1867 the Canadians formed a Confederation with a central government in control of their own affairs.

Land exploration had reached Winnipeg in 1812 by wagon and canoe, but by 1870 there were scarcely 10,000 pioneers in the prairie lands. Then with the arrival of steamboats on rivers and lakes the land was rapidly opened up. By 1885, when the Canadian Pacific Railway was completed, the prairie was becoming productive and the real pioneering was over – unification was complete.

Canada has spectacular scenery of great contrast and grandeur; there are huge mountain ranges, dense forests, wide expanses of prairie, tremendous rivers, cataracts and lakes twice the size of England. One thirteenth of Canada is fresh water. There are four of the Great Lakes, Superior, Huron, Erie and Ontario, partly in Canadian territory and many others completely in Canada. The Mackenzie river flows 2,500 miles to the Arctic while the most important waterway in the world, the St. Lawrence, drains the Great Lakes and is the main route from the Atlantic to the interior. The far northern coast is a network of peninsulas and inlets with Hudson Bay thrusting south like an enormous inland sea. The coastline is rugged both east and west and is one of the longest in the world and there is an abundance of fish.

Geographically Canada falls into natural divisions, each with a distinctive character. The whole area is covered by a dense air network considerably cheaper than Europe. Transcontinental rail travel is still popular and long distance buses operate to far-removed points.

Starting on the Pacific coast there is British Columbia with Vancouver, third largest city of Canada and a great port and commercial centre. The climate is the country's kindest, so warm and moist that there are luxuriant forests and gardens making it the 'Suncoast' for vacations. Away inland are the Rocky Mountains, a magnificent range of snow-capped peaks and waterfalls. There is Banff National Park, the oldest of the conservation areas. Spreading eastward is the Great Central Plain of the prairie provinces of Alberta, Saskatchewan and Manitoba. This is big-sky country, the "breadbasket" of Canada. The black loam soil produces more wheat than anywhere else in the world. Cattle, sheep and horses are raised in large numbers. Calgary is there, the home of the world-famous stampede. Edmonton is the centre of the national oil industry, while Regina is the original home of the Mounties. Moose Jaw is a part of the classic prairie scene and a centre for Indian culture. To realise the distances one should remember that Winnipeg, the world's grain market and patron of symphony orchestra and ballet, is equidistant from the Atlantic and Pacific oceans. This makes for extreme weather with winter blizzards, heavy spring rain and very hot summers.

The Canadian Shield of ancient rock covers half of Canada from Hudson Bay to the Atlantic. At the heart of this is the province of Ontario; the southern part is the most populated part of the country (two out of three people live within 100 miles of the U.S.–Canada border). Here it is warm enough for crops such as tobacco, peaches and grapes. This is maple country from which comes maple syrup, the national delicacy. Toronto is a sophisticated urbanised area of skyscrapers, 16 lane highways and suburban-density living which makes it financially and culturally the second largest city. The timeless wonder of Niagara Falls is situated to the south – easily accessible for tourists from Canada and the United States. At Kingston the St. Lawrence begins with the spectacle of the 1,000 Islands – small densely wooded islands contrasting with the expanse of Lake Ontario. The Rideau Canal of 1831 runs north to Ottawa – a reminder of the hostility that once existed across the St. Lawrence to the U.S. border. Ottawa was chosen as the capital in 1857 as the meeting place of English and French cultures: both languages are officially used.

In contrast Quebec is the French province and Montreal has become the largest French-speaking city after Paris. In spite of the rigours of the severe winters, this has become the pulsating commercial centre on the grand scale with its miles of modern all-weather underground shopping and its historic Notre Dame Church, the largest in America. The French character of the entire province has determined a way of life distinct from the rest of Canada. Quebec City is no less unique in being a natural citadel and was the key to the interior of the North American continent for centuries.

The Maritime Provinces of New Brunswick, Nova Scotia, Prince Edward Island and Newfoundland are places of great rugged landscapes, virgin forests and fishing communities. St. John's, Newfoundland, is the oldest city founded by Europeans in North America and also boasts Gander, the large international airport.

The most extreme temperatures are experienced around the 60° Parallel in the Yukon and Northwest Territories. This is a region of lofty mountains and swift rivers with a sparse population that first attracted the outside world in Gold Rush days. Although remote, Whitehorse has jet links daily and Yellowknife is a modern fast-growing town. There are some 11,500 Eskimos in these Arctic regions scattered among the towns and settlements like Unuvik who are gradually being educated to take an active part in modern life.

The other ethnic minority is the group of about 185,000 native Indians who have fitted into the life of their white neighbours in many places, but who have an increasing interest in their own early history, and pride in their culture. More and more interest is being taken by Canadians in the way of life and hardships of the early settlers and pioneer life is being reconstructed in living museums like Upper Canada Village.

Canada is endowed with great advantages to offset the difficulties of distance and severe climate. There are 270,000 square miles of farmland and three times that area of forests. The mineral resources are rich. Canada leads the world in the production of nickel and asbestos, is second in uranium and platinum, and also produces magnesium, iron, coal, petroleum and natural gas. With unlimited supplies of water power, nine-tenths of the electric power used can be provided.

The Great Outdoors is truly Canada. The Trans-Canada Highway stretches 4,860 miles and there are local Highway Routes such as the Yellowhead Route passing through sixteen National Parks and the Heritage Route that links two cultures through Ontario and Quebec. There are unlimited recreational facilities for all outdoor activities like camping, hunting, angling, sailing, swimming and skiing. Because of the long cold winters, the great national game is ice hockey and skiing and skating are for everyone.

The frontiers have been pushed back and the great resources opened up due to the boundless energy and imagination of man. The accepted standards of civilised life and comforts have been attained, but there is still a frontier where the potential is as yet untapped and the future could be exciting when new solutions have been devised.

CONTENTS

BRITISH COLUMBIA

Nestling below the mountain playgrounds of Grouse, Seymour and Hollyburn, Vancouver is surrounded to the north and west by Howe Sound and English Bay, and to the east and south by the fertile farmlands of the Fraser Valley and the Fraser Delta. The city's history is a short one: from a small milltown to a metropolis in less than a century. 1791 was the year the first European sailed into the Strait of Georgia but José Maria Narvaez failed to discover the wooded narrows now spanned by the Lions Gate Bridge as he anchored at Point Grey in the English Bay. Just a year later Capt. George Vancouver entered this great natural harbour and named the inlet after his friend, Sir Harry Burrard. It was not until 1862 that the first white settlers arrived and Sam Brighouse, Willie Hailstone and John Morton–"Three Greenhorn Englishmen"–bought for about one dollar an acre, land which today comprises most of Vancouver's West End, one of the richest square miles in North America. Sawmills appeared and in April of 1886 the waterfront shanty town was incorporated as the City of Vancouver. Two months later a forest fire raced towards the new-born city and within one hour the fire had destroyed most of it. Work started again and by the end of the same year the city had 14 office blocks, 52 stores, 9 saloons, 1 church, 23 hotels and 5,000 people for whom the future looked much brighter. CP Railroads had to extend its terminal by 12½ miles and on May 23, 1887, the first passenger train from the east reached Vancouver. Engine CPR 374 *right bottom* is now on display at Kitsilano Beach.

The Lions Gate Bridge *left*, little short of one mile, was to provide access to the new development of West and North Vancouver across the Burrard Inlet and was officially opened in 1938. Stanley Park at the south end of the bridge, with its impressive 1,000 acres of forest, today provides recreation for young and old alike. Two beautiful lakes, Lost Lagoon and Beaver Lake, nestle among hemlock, cedar and giant stands of Douglas fir. To the south the park invites magnificent views of the downtown Vancouver skyline *overleaf*.

Top right. Cheerful B. Chapman of No. 7 Fire Hall, 1090 Haro, is part of a most modern and efficient Vancouver Fire Department determined to prevent a re-occurrence of the 1886 disaster.

Busy Cambie *top left* leads downtown and into Robson Street, which became Robson Strasse in the 1950's when Germans and other European immigrants added some continental flair by opening up cake-shops, Viennese coffee-parlours and other specialty shops.

The residential area along Kitsilano Beach *centre left*.

Totem poles in Stanley Park facing the always impressive Vancouver skyline across the coal harbour *below and bottom left*.

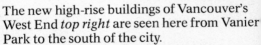

The new high-rise buildings of Vancouver's West End *top right* are seen here from Vanier Park to the south of the city.

A bird's eye view from the Sheraton Landmark *bottom right* shows Robson Strasse and the English Bay in the background.

Horseshoe Bay *overleaf*, not far from Vancouver, serves as a ferry port for travellers to Vancouver Island.

Ships in English Bay *above* rest at anchor in the evening sun, while in Gastown *right* the busy life continues. Gastown was named after John "Gassy Jack" Deighton, a Yorkshireman who arrived in Canada in the 1860's and opened a public house. His tombstone in New Westminster bears his words: "I have done well since I came here". Gastown eventually became a slum but was rescued in the late 1960's and is today Vancouver's trendiest area.

False Creek and Burrard Bridge *top*.

Vanier Park creates a perfect setting for the H.R.MacMillan Planetarium *above* south of downtown Vancouver. In the background Grouse and Seymour Mountains can be seen.

Chinatown *left,* claimed to be the second largest Chinese community in North America outside San Francisco, offers a wide variety of colours, exotic shops, oriental food-markets and restaurants.

19

East of Vancouver, highway Number 3 leads to Manning Provincial Park *below and bottom left* and later via highway Number 97 to the Okanagan Valley *centre left*, famous for its rich fruit orchards. Penticton, Summerland, Peachland, Kelowna and Vernon are just a few of the places passed before entering the lovely Coldstream Valley *left*.

A cabin among the trees *bottom right* near the entrance to Mount Robson Provincial Park.

Kimberley, Canada's highest city and since 1972 "The Bavarian City of the Canadian Rockies" entertains its guests the Bavarian way with high-spots of a "Winterfest" during the second week of February and a "Julifest" on the third weekend of July. All summer long the residents of Kimberley wear authentic garb in the "Platzl" area to provide that extra bit of atmosphere for the visitors. The world's largest lead and zinc mine offers tours while Fort Steele and Peckham Lake *top right* are within easy reach.

uf. A sawmill on the shore of Lake near the city of Nelson.

20

During the 1960's a Kootenay town of the 1890-1905 period was created as the pictures on this page show, in the Fort Steele Historic Park. Fort Steele, overlooking the Kootenay River and at an altitude of 2,500 feet, was named after Samuel Benfield–"Sam" Steele–who was a legend in his own colourful lifetime. As a policeman and soldier he appeared at most Canadian trouble spots and in Canada's wars overseas, for over half a century. Sternwheelers on the Kootenay River linked Fort Steele with the railroad at Jennings, Montana, during the silver, lead and zinc boom at nearby Kimberley and Moyie. However, the fort deteriorated when the Canadian Pacific Railroad by-passed the town in favour of Cranbrook some 12 miles to the south-west. After World War II Fort Steele was a ghost town and only in 1961 was it designated a historic park. The Wild Horse Theatre presents live Gay Nineties entertainment, stagecoach rides and performances by a six-horse hitch from Fort Steele's own herd of Clydesdales add interest during the summer months.

Transcontinental transport is undertaken on a huge scale by road as *top right* on the Yellowhead highway below Mount Robson, the highest peak in the Canadian Rockies, or by rail as in the picture *bottom right* of CN railways here crossing the North Thompson river near the town of Blue River.

Highway Number 16, or Yellowhead Highway as it is better known, follows the Skeena River right up to Prince Rupert *below,* from where ferry services operate to the Queen Charlotte Islands, Vancouver Island and to Alaska, U.S.A. At Hazelton along the river Skeena *left* the reconstructed Indian village of K'san is well worth a visit.

Pavillion Lake near Lillooet *centre left.*
The mighty Frazer River near Lillooet *bottom left.*
Evening over Lillooet Lake showing Garibaldi Provincial Park in the distance *top right.*
An aerial view of the Rocky Mountains *bottom right.*

"To realize Victoria" wrote Rudyard Kipling, "you must take all that the eye admires in Bournemouth, Torquay, the Isle of Wight, the Happy Valley in Hong Kong, the Doon, Sorrento, Camp's Bay, add reminiscences of the Thousand Islands and arrange the whole around the Bay of Naples with some Himalayas for the background". A very apt description of British Columbia's capital. For the tourists there are double-decker London buses and the Tally-Ho carriages, fish and chips or roast beef and yorkshire pudding at the Olde English Inn *right,* cricket in Beacon Hill Park and lots of British souvenir shops. The city and its people are mainly of British origin and a bit of Old England and the Old Empire can be found around every corner. Boats gather in preparation for the yearly "Swift Sure" yacht race, overlooked in the harbour by the illuminated Parliament Buildings *above.*

Tofino Harbour *far right* is situated on the Pacific coast, north of the Pacific Rim National Park.

Wippletree Junction *above* offers antiques and souvenirs from bygone days while back in Victoria, Craigflower Manor *left* represents a Hudson's Bay Company farm which once supplied Fort Victoria with vegetables and fruit as well as meat and dairy produce. Today it is a museum and a national historic site containing the furnishings and possessions of Kenneth MacKenzie, the Hudson's Bay Company representative who once lived in it.

29

Butchart's Gardens *top left,* just 20 km from Victoria, is a 35 acre garden site created by Mr. and Mrs. Butchart. Standing atop the main lookout, high above the Sunken Garden, the visitor finds it hard to believe this was once a quarry for Robert Pim Butchart's cement plant. Nearly 75 years later, the sight fills even the frequent visitor with awe. Starting in 1904, with a few scattered sweet peas and some roses, Jennie Butchart began to create one of the world's most magnificent gardens. Mr. and Mrs. Butchart named their gardens "Benvenuto", the Italian for "welcome" and encouraged everyone to come, she said, for, "the flowers are fleeting and everyone should have a chance to enjoy them".

The Pacific Rim National Park, stretching from Port Renfrew to Tofino, consists of three parts: Long Beach *above and bottom left* which incorporates a rain-forest *centre left,* Barkley Sound, including the Broken Islands Group, and the West Coast Trail, a wilderness between Bamfield and Port Renfrew. The trail snakes south for 75 km and was established for shipwrecked sailors who could walk inland, pick up the trail and so return to civilisation.

Opposite. An Indian mask in the provincial museum within the Heritage Court complex, Victoria.

Barkerville typified Cariboo gold towns–a jumble of log shanties, saloons and false-fronted stores on stilts along a single narrow and muddy street. Soon it boasted of being "the largest town west of Chicago and north of San Francisco". Boots cost $50 a pair, soap $1.25 a bar, and a dance with a buxom 'hurdy-gurdy' girl cost a man $10 a whirl. Wild it was; yet travelling actors played Shakespeare in the Theatre Royal and the peace was kept by British justice, personified in the stern but fair Judge Matthew Baillie Begbie. Wiped out by fire on September 16th, 1886, Barkerville was rebuilt, but its wealth was already fading. Miners drifted away and though Barkerville's fortunes rose and fell with the price of gold, the town never regained its former glory. When the Barkerville Restoration Committee began its task in 1958, only 15 of some 120 original buildings were standing. Hotels, houses, saloons, butchers' and blacksmiths' shops and a theatre were gradually reconstructed while faithfully keeping to every detail of the period 1869–1885. St. Saviour's Anglican Church at the end of the main street *bottom left,* was built of whipsawn local timber and square nails, with window glass freighted in from Victoria.

Top left Barkerville Hotel.
Below The Caribou Sentinel printing office.
Bottom View of Main Street.

Opposite are some impressions of the fun, excitement and dust at the annual Prince George Professional Rodeo which is held in early June.

33

1,520 miles, or 2,300 km., from "Mile-O" city, Dawson Creek, to Fairbanks in Alaska, stretches a windy, narrow and dusty road called with affection, by many, the "Alaska Highway". Many who have travelled on this highway come back again to drive this experience of a life-time. "Wash-outs" and "freeze-ups" are part of it; the dust gets everywhere, windscreens often get broken and so do head-lights, which are essential to be seen through the clouds of dust. One asks in vain for a weather forecast upon arrival at Toad River, and a friendly gas-station attendant explains that there is no radio or television service in this region. But during a stop along Muncho Lake – Mile 456 – overleaf, one may enjoy boating on the quiet lake and hearty steak at the log-cabin. Making friends with the people along the highway makes this trip even more memorable, a journey which soon may become a journey of the past, for the proposed oil pipeline will require a "proper" road.

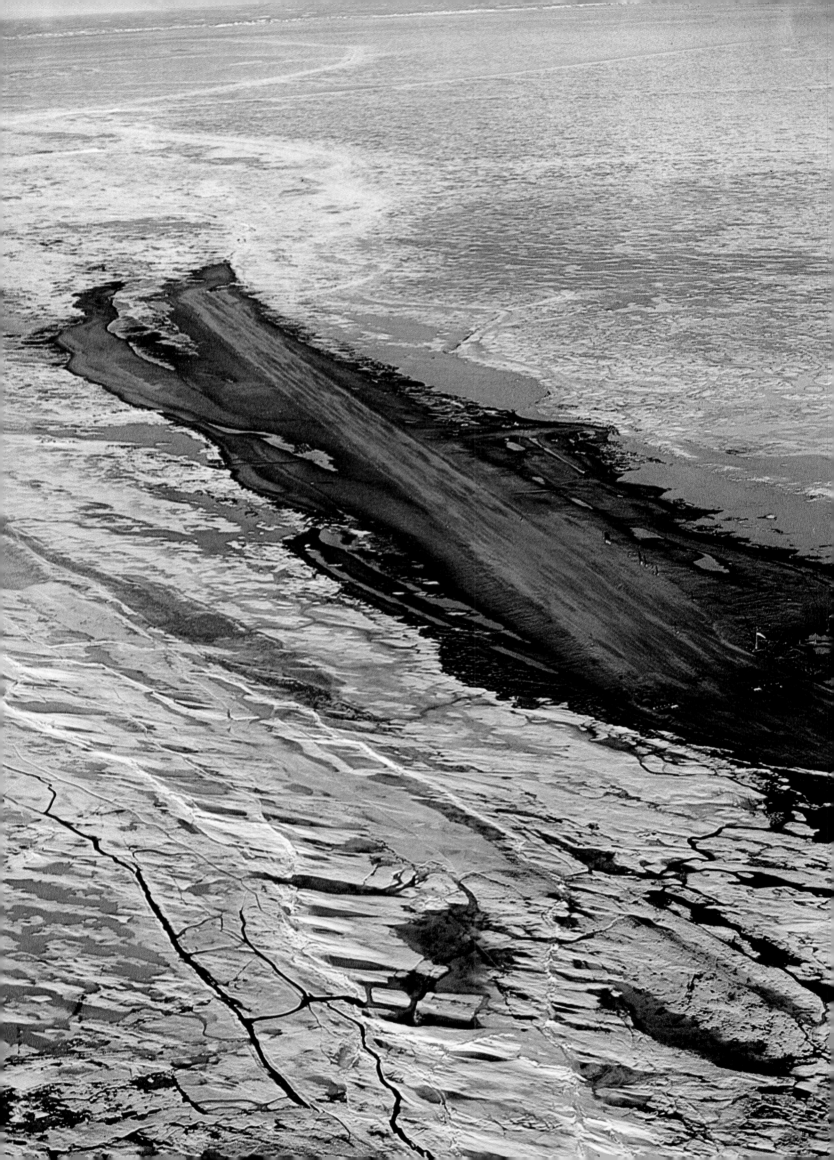

NORTHWEST TERRITORIES

The Northwest Territories lie to the north of the prairie provinces of Alberta, Saskatchewan and Manitoba, and east of the Yukon. They make up a truly vast area and include the islands known as the Arctic Archipelago.

The biggest problem that has to be faced is, as might be expected, the weather. As the pictures on these pages, and overleaf, show, life in this part of Canada is normally hard for man and beast alike. Surprisingly, however, some parts of the Northwest Territories can be very warm during the summer and outdoor activities such as sailing, camping and fishing are popular.

Left Landing strip in sea ice.
Right Aerial view of Churchill.
Above, top, top right and centre right
Eskimo life in the Northwest Territories.

ALBERTA

Moraine Lake *top left* in the Valley of the Ten Peaks and still in British Columbia, opens the gate to the Canadian Rockies from the west. Via the Trans-Canada Highway, Bow River comes into sight, here seen with Mt. Eisenhower in the background *bottom left*, before entering Banff *bottom right*, a busy summer and winter resort. The hoodoos *below* along a trail 4 kms. east of the town of Banff are light-coloured natural pillars made

of glacial till (clay, sand, gravel and boulders), held tightly together by the lime of the waters coming down from the glaciers. The till has resisted erosion and so the hoodoos have been shaped over the centuries. Along the David Thompson Highway lies Ram River Falls *left centre*. Near Jasper and en-route to Maligne Lake, a deer grazes above Medicine Lake *top right*.

Peyto viewpoint near the Bow Pass on the Icefield Parkway opens up magnificent views of Peyto Lake *overleaf* and the ranges to the north.

The animals of the Rocky Mountains are an interesting mixture of prairie, forest and arctic forms. Each has its own particular requirements and can only survive where these exist. In summer, the large grazing animals range throughout the mountains, each seeking its own preferred habitat. Mountain goats and bighorn sheep favour high alpine areas, elk and deer the lush forest meadows, while chipmunks, ground-squirrels and coyotes are not so particular where they feed. The black bear, which may in fact be black, brown or even yellow, can be seen by park visitors as it forages for food in open meadows or on mountain slopes. The grizzly bear normally inhabits the more remote regions of the Rocky Mountains. National Park regulations forbid feeding or molesting any wildlife; bears in particular are dangerous and should be left alone.

Rocky Mountain Poppies at Lake Louise *left*.

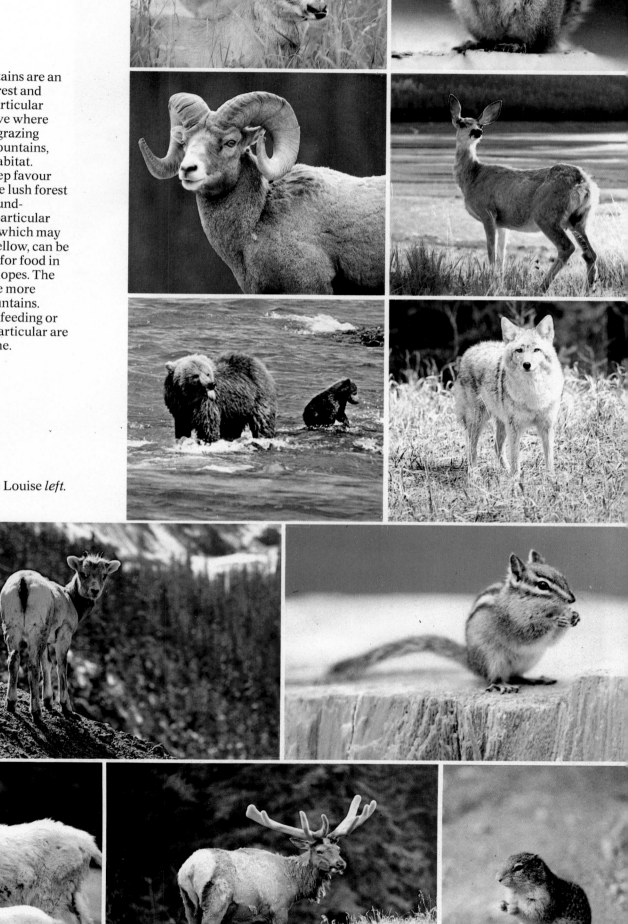

The Athabasca River *both pages* appears in fascinating journals and records relating stories of pioneer travellers through Jasper. Gold-seekers, fur brigades, and explorers sought routes to the Pacific coast. Some of them fought the currents of the Athabasca River to the Whirlpool and worked out a passage to the Columbia River and Boat Encampment on the Big Bend. There they met brigades from the Pacific and together inaugurated the first "express" service between Hudson Bay and the west coast. Today the Icefield Parkway runs alongside the river and, for the more adventurous, raft tours are available. The Athabasca Falls *top left* command spectacular vistas from two viewpoints and are within easy reach of Jasper.

The Columbia Icefield *overleaf* covers a large area of the Canadian Rockies. Twelve of the twenty-five highest mountains are found in the Icefield. Every day during the summer season a fleet of glacier-travel vehicles operates from terminals to a point about four kilometres up the Athabasca Glacier. For most people this will be their first experience of such a ride; it is not every day that one has a chance to travel on an ice cube some 350 metres deep and nine kilometres long.

Alberta Number 2 highway–this is the longest south-north highway in Alberta. 750 kms. of road runs from Carway on the U.S. border north through Cardstone, Fort McLeod, Calgary, Red Deer, Ponoka *bottom right and below*, Edmonton *overleaf*, along

Lesser Slave Lake *left*, beside the rapeseed fields of Fairview *top right* and through the farmlands around Beaverlodge *centre right*. Eventually it crosses, at Tupper, into British Columbia.

dmonton is Alberta's capital and largest city
ith a metropolitan population of more than
lf a million. It is a dynamic city which still
tains the friendly Western Canadian
vour of an earlier, less hurried era. The
78 Commonwealth Games brought
ternational interest to this fast expanding
etropolis. Downtown Edmonton *top and*
ft changes its silhouette from year to year
d Jasper Avenue *top right* comes to a
andstill during rush hour. The Provincial
useum *centre right* was completed in 1967
mark Canada's Centennial Year–it offers
splays illustrating Alberta's natural and
man history and exhibits depict early
ative Indian life, pioneer settlement,
ology and the ecological zones of the
ovince. Muttart Conservatory *below*
presents a controlled environment growing
ea unlike any other in North America; each
the pyramids contains the flora of a
ecific climatic zone. The 150 acre campus
the University of Alberta *bottom right* is
e province's major degree-granting
stitution with a student population of
out 20,000.

The Annual "Touring Tin" rally from Calgary to Banff

Sixty kilometres to the west, the Rocky Mountains provide a backdrop to Calgary–a young and rich city renowned for its dry westerly chinook, bright sunshine, low humidity and, of course, the annual Calgary Stampede. In 1914 oil was discovered almost on the doorstep of the city and today there are more than 400 companies in Calgary directly involved in the oil industry while 28 major oil companies have their head offices in the city. The modern skyline is dominated by the Calgary Tower (191 m.) which houses an observation deck and a revolving restaurant, presenting an incredible panorama of the city, prairie, the foothills and the Rockies.

55

The Calgary Stampede *these pages and overleaf* – the greatest outdoor show on earth; for ten days in July Calgary lives it up. Dancing in the streets, Indians in colourful regalia, the thunder of hooves, Mounties and pretty girls, flapjacks and coffee at the curbside, is all part of it. There are grandstand shows, fireworks, livestock exhibits, a huge fun-fair and a village with Stony, Sarcee, Blood and Blackfoot Indians. Cowboys from all over Canada and the United States compete for over $225,000 in prize money during the richest rodeo in the world. Daily events include saddle and bareback bronco busting, Brahma bull and buffalo riding, a wild-horse race, steer wrestling, calf roping and wrestling, wild-cow milking, the world famous Royal Canadian Mounted Police Musical Ride plus the most hair-raising event, which was invented in Alberta; the Chuck Wagon Race in which four wagons, 20 riders and 32 horses speed for the finish.

The Valley of the Dinosaurs *right* near Drumheller, is an unusual scenic valley, created by massive glacial action millions of years ago. Once tropical marshland for the giant reptiles of pre-history, it has now become a naturalist's paradise.

Dinosaur Provincial Park *above and centre left*, one of the most significant natural and historical Parks of Canada, is located 40 kilometres northeast of Brooks along the Red Deer River. The park is noted for its spectacular badland scenery as well as its dinosaur quarries and displays. A major portion of the park is restricted and is only accessible by means of a guided bus tour–in addition there are self-guiding nature trails and walks through areas of historical and geological interest.

Writing-On-Stone Provincial Park *left* lies in the short grass prairie region of Alberta, some 41 kilometres east of Coutts and a stone's throw away from the U.S. border. The old Northwest Mounted Police Post is being reconstructed on its original site within the park. The park itself was named after Indian petroglyphs (rock carvings) and pictographs (rock paintings), inscribed on the massive sandstone outcrops. The combination of rock formations (hoodoos, formed by wind and rain erosion on soft sandstone), the Milk River Valley and the nearby Sweetgrass Hills in the background provide an exceptional scenic area.

Waterton Lakes National Park, here represented by Red Rock Canyon *left* and Waterton township *right* fronts its fortress-like mountains on the open Alberta prairie that borders the park. Indians inhabited some areas of the territory for 3,000 years, and it was the easily defended stronghold of the powerful Blackfoot Confederacy when western Canada was first settled by white men. For this reason the area was virtually unknown to whites until Lieutenant Thomas Blakiston of the Palliser Expedition explored it in 1858. He named the lakes after Charles Waterton, a well known 18th century English naturalist. Glacier Park in Montana and Waterton Lakes National Park were joined in 1932 as the world's first international peace park.

Medicine Hat *below* arrived at its name– so the story goes–when, years ago, Cree and Blackfoot fought on the bank of the river here. The Cree held their own until their medicine man suddenly deserted them, losing his head-dress. Obviously a bad omen, as the Cree surrendered and were killed. The site of the tragedy was called "saamis", an Indian word meaning "medicine man's hat", later to become Medicine Hat.

SASKATCHEWAN

The land of the wide horizons or "Big Sky Country" *below and right* stretches from the U.S. border to the Northwest Territories. Until entering the Confederation in 1905, the large province, in fact, formed part of the Northwest Territories. Under its broad skies are virgin grasslands and wilderness forests, rich grainfields *left* and silent streams, busy cities and scenic badlands, roaring waterfalls and prosperous woodlands. Saskatchewan is Canada's major wheat-growing province and its livestock industry is also of great importance. Minerals found within the province include gold, silver and cadmium.

Watering these huge fields is no easy task, but done "Saskatchewan Style" it looks easy, *overleaf.*

Regina, a prairie city, was once a settlement called "Pile of Bones" and has been a capital since 1882, first of the Northwest Territories, later (in 1905) of Saskatchewan. The city's heart is Wascana Centre, a 2,000-acre parkland in which the Legislative Building, an adaptation of English Renaissance architecture with elements of Louis XVI, is set off by the blue prairie sky and colourful formal gardens *left and right.* The new city hall *below and centre left* was opened in the summer of 1977.

Six bridges span the South Saskatchewan River at Saskatoon, Saskatchewan's second largest city *below left,* opening the way to the city centre with its wide and tree-lined roads. The famous Bessborough Hotel still remains as a landmark amongst the new modern office blocks, providing magnificent views across the city and the river.

A thunder-storm passes over Halkett Lake *overleaf* in the Prince Albert National Park in the north of the province.

MANITOBA

When thinking of Manitoba one pictures a province full of sunshine leaping and sparkling on the surface of 100,000 lakes and rivers, cool shaded forest paths and gentle rolling farmlands inhabited by an exceptionally hospitable people. They give one a genuine welcome to their ethnic festivals: at Gimli on Lake Winnipeg during the midsummer Islendingadagurinn of the first and largest Icelandic community outside Iceland *right*; at Dauphin during the annual July celebration of Canada's Ukrainian population; at Steinbach *top left, below, centre left and below left* during the Pioneer

Days held in July in the reconstructed Mennonite town first settled by Russians in 1874. It is a region that unites people from far away places, bringing them together to share song, dance and food from their different cultures.

Clear Lake, Riding Mountain National Park *overleaf*. This National Park is an "island" within the prairie, and dramatic evidence of Manitoba's geological past. The near 8,000 m. high mountain is part of the Manitoba Escarpment, a jagged, 1,500 km. ridge that winds across North Dakota, Manitoba and Saskatchewan. Clear Lake, fourteen kilometres long, is most certainly the focal point of Riding Mountain National Park.

Winnipeg, Manitoba's capital *above and overleaf*, has the good fortune to be a rare blend of the sophisticated east of Canada and the openhearted friendliness of its western neighbours. It is located in the heart of the country, and attracts a wealth and variety of culture, entertainment and business. Spring and summer visitors enjoy, in particular, the riverboat and cruiseship trips up and down the Red and Assiniboine Rivers, which offer spectacular sunset cruises and dancing under the stars. The Manitoba Museum of Man and Nature *right* is one of Canada's finest museums. At this museum one can enjoy exploring not only the past, but the world we live in now and the world we will be living in tomorrow.

The Manitoba Legislature *above* was built (from 1913-19) in classic Greek style. Atop the dome can be seen the famous Golden Boy, a 4.12m. gilded bronze statue of a running youth. Dominating the base of the elegant marble staircase *top* leading from the vestibule to the antehall beneath the dome of the Legislative building are two enormous bronze buffaloes. Millions of buffaloes once roamed the prairies but were hunted to near extinction. This magnificent animal is now the emblem of Manitoba and is prominent in Manitoba's Coat-of-Arms. The Winnipeg Mint *left* is a branch of the Royal Canadian Mint and is the most modern mint in the world, designed so that the public are able to see the "magic" of money making.

77

ONTARIO

Lake-of-the-Woods *far left* extends across the most westerly 80 kms. of Ontario and into Manitoba. Southwards it stretches about twice this distance, as far as the United States. It covers approx. 2,300 square kilometres with no less than 14,000 islands.

A typical Ontario farm *top* near Thunder Bay. Thunder Bay is the western terminus of the St. Lawrence – Great Lakes Waterway.

To avoid the *sault* (old French word meaning "rapids") where the St. Mary's River leaves Lake Superior in order to join Lake Huron, and to overcome the 6.50 m. difference in water level between the two lakes, the Soo Locks, part of the St. Lawrence seaway, *above* were constructed at Sault Ste. Marie.

INCO *left and top left* International Nickel's mills, smelters and refineries recover 15 elements, including nickel, copper, gold and silver. The Ontario Division's plants form the Free World's largest integrated nickel-copper mining and refining complex, with 5 concentrators (mills), a copper-nickel separation plant and an iron ore recovery plant in the Sudbury District and an electrolytic nickel refinery at Port Colborne. In addition, the company operates a mine and mill at Shebandowan, about 90 kms. west of Thunder Bay.

81

The most striking feature of Toronto, Ontario's capital, as one approaches the city is its massive skyline of tall banks, hotels, and office buildings. The city's ever-changing skyline is dominated by four towering office-commercial complexes bearing the names of Canada's leading banks. The tallest of the quadrumvirate of bank skyscrapers is the 72-storey Bank of Montreal Building, which is covered in white marble imported from Italy. The Commerce Court (57 storeys) is a stainless steel skyscraper with some 7,400 windows of double-glazed reflective glass. The dazzling Royal Bank Plaza features twin towers covered with $250,000 in gold leaf. The Toronto Dominion Centre consists of three buildings and was, on completion in 1967, Toronto's first super-development. But the most impressive construction is the CN-Tower, the tallest self-supporting structure in the world. At 553·33 metres the tower has been confirmed as the world's tallest freestanding

structure by the Guinness Book of Records. It provides not only the most efficient transmission facilities for television and radio, but also features a revolving restaurant at the 350m. level and two observation decks at 341m. and 445m. with potential views across the city *overleaf* and Lake Ontario. Many regard Toronto's daringly designed City Hall *above and bottom left* as the catalyst to the city's construction and cultural booms. Opened in 1965, the City Hall consists of a white dome nestling between two curved 27 and 20 storey towers. The structure not only houses municipal administrative offices but also features spacious Nathan Phillips Square, a nine-acre open space in the core of the city, containing green lawns and a pool that becomes a skating rink in the winter. As a year-round meeting place for visitors, businessmen and residents alike, City Hall truly deserves its claim to fame as the symbol of Toronto, an Indian word meaning "place of meeting".

Ontario Place top left, is an exciting showcase of the province, standing high over Lake Ontario on three man-made islands and providing 96 acres for family entertainment. Open from late spring to mid-fall, Ontario Place has an outdoor amphitheatre that seats 8,000 people and offers free entertainment from symphony concerts to rock shows. A domed cinesphere houses the world's largest curved film screen and theatres, restaurants, boutiques, children's playgrounds and a marina add to the many attractions.

Casa Loma *above*, a 100-room mansion built between 1911 and 1914 by a Toronto soldier, financier and industrialist, is now operated as a sightseeing attraction. With secret panels, hidden stairway and spooky turrets, this fairy-tale castle is an ideal subject for the photographer.

Eaton Centre *far left* opened its gates in 1977 and must rank amongst the finest shopping areas in the world.

Sheraton Centre and Hotel Toronto, *top*.

There are more than 100 parks throughout Metropolitan Toronto – perhaps the most complete is the Toronto Island Park which can be reached by old-fashioned ferry transport which leaves at frequent intervals from the harbour below the Toronto Harbour Castle Hilton *centre left*. This is a favourite getaway spot for Toronto's residents, especially in summer when families happily comply with the island's posted request to "Please Walk On The Grass."

From Ontario Place it is just a short step to Exhibition Place, home of the Canadian National Exhibition (CNE), Canada's annual celebration, Toronto's biggest party and the world's largest fair. At the same time it is the oldest annual exhibition in the world. From Mid-August to Labour Day it is non-stop action, with competitions, floral displays, demonstrations, farm animals, dog shows, lumberjack races, grandstand shows, aquarama displays, powerboat races, fly pasts; plus "dodgem" cars, roller coasters, bingo, fun houses and, of course, fireworks every night.

Kingston *top left, right and bottom right* lies at the eastern end of Lake Ontario where it flows into the St. Lawrence River, and was developed from a military installation. Old Fort Henry *centre left and below left* stands on a hill overlooking the city and has today become a major tourist attraction. Throughout the summer months university students *below*, wearing nineteenth-century uniforms and carrying weapons of the period, drill with smart precision for the pleasure of thousands of visitors, re-enacting a proud and colourful part of the country's history.

Near Ivy Lea, the 1,000 Islands International Bridge *left* spans the St. Lawrence River. Located between the spans, on Hill Island and still on Canadian soil, is the unique Skytown observation tower. Farther downriver another bridge, the Ogdensburg International Bridge *bottom right*, crosses over to the United States at Johnstown.

Windsor *bottom left*, Canada's southernmost city, is the nation's fifth biggest industrial producer and, like its neighbour Detroit, a major manufacturer of automobiles. The Dieppe Gardens on the Windsor waterfront across from Detroit, commemorate the Dieppe raid of August 19th, 1942, in which a local battalion, the Essex Scottish, suffered heavy casualties.

Niagara Falls *above, centre left and top right*, where the mighty Niagara River plunges over the escarpment into a deep gorge, is one of the world's most spectacular shows of natural beauty. The Canadian Horseshoe Falls measure 671 metres across and are an impressive 54 metres high. First described by a priest who travelled with La Salle, the Rev. Louis Hennepin, the falls have attracted honeymooners, stunt-men and tourists since the early 1800's. The river also provides, at this point, much of the hydroelectric power for Ontario and New York.

As planning proceeded in the 1950's for the development of the power and navigation facilities in the International Rapids section of the St. Lawrence River, it became apparent that a great deal of early history of the area would disappear under the waters of the head-pond to be formed. The land to be lost included that settled by the loyalists in 1784, as well as Crysler Farm, the site of one of the decisive battles of the War of 1812 in Canada. The St. Lawrence Parks Commission was formed by the Government of Ontario to safeguard and enhance the scenic beauty and historic association with the region.

Upper Canada Village *both pages* was created by bringing together selected buildings, furnishings, tools and equipment, and arranging them to portray settings that could have been found in rural Eastern Ontario before 1867. In many parts of the village men and women may be seen busy at tasks from that earlier era. They bring alive the work of the blacksmith, cabinetmaker, mill operator, cheesemaker, farmer and also demonstrates the skills of the housewife at the spinning wheel, loom, quilting frame and the wood stove.

Upper Canada Village is situated near Morrisburg, and village produce as well as souvenirs can be obtained from the Village Store, while free stage-coach rides and barge-trips on the canal entertain young and old alike.

"...In the judgment of Her Majesty the City of Ottawa combines more advantages than any other place in Canada for the permanent seat of the future government...and is selected by Her Majesty accordingly." With these historic words the choice was made in 1857 by Queen Victoria, thus ending the aspirations of Montreal, Toronto, Quebec Cit and Kingston of becoming Canada's capital. The construction of the Parliament Buildings was started in 1859 and still today the three huge Victorian Gothic buildings dominate th city from Parliament Hill *centre left and below.* The Confederation Hall *top left* and the Senate Chamber *right* are but a few of the magnificent interiors within the Parliament Buildings. Visitors are welcome to look around.

A night-time view of downtown Ottawa *left* shows the National Arts Centre *lower left* an *overleaf* another night-time view shows the world-famous Château Laurier, and to the le the Parliament Buildings. The famous hotel, built of granite and Indiana sandstone, with towers, turrets and steeply pitched copper roofs, was opened in 1912.

n Parliament Hill, the Peace Tower soars
2 metres above the Eternal Flame *top right*.
he centre block, replacing the original
uilding which burned down in 1916, more
oberly resembles a mediaeval guildhall.
oday Ottawa shares its old and new
eritage with all its visitors and an officer of
e Royal Canadian Mounted Police is
ways on duty outside Parliament to give
dvice and help to tourists from all parts of
e globe *left*. Changing the Guard *centre*
ght is another daily event that draws the
owds while in Major's Hill Park *bottom*
ght, just around the corner from
arliament Hill and behind the Château
aurier, autumn leaves frame the views
cross the Ottawa River.

e frozen Rideau Canal *above* is used every
nter by about 500,000 skaters – the 7 km.
g rink from the National Arts Centre to
rleton University provides six activity
tres, each having ample parking,
taurants and skate sharpening facilities.

QUEBEC

Greater Montreal is a city of almost three million people and the second largest French speaking metropolis in the world. It ranks among the largest seaports and is, in fact, the largest inland seaport in the world. Situated on an island, the city is connected to the mainland by 11 vehicular bridges, 5 railway bridges and one tunnel. Montreal is Canada's largest city; there are more than 550 churches–almost as many as in Rome–and there are more bars in Montreal than in almost any other North American city. The city's joie de vivre sometimes seems at odds with its religious character. Photos on this page depict: the Royal Bank of Canada Building *left,* Complex Desjardin shopping centre *below,* St. Catherine Street by night *top right* and Place du Canada *bottom right.*

Overleaf is a view of the business section of downtown Montreal seen from Mount Royal

Mount Royal, a former volcano, rises 230m. above sea level and affords a magnificent view of the city *overleaf*. In winter the terrace of Beaver Lake Pavilion changes into a skating rink *right*. There are also ski trails, toboggan hills and horse-drawn sleighs. An illuminated cross 30m. high stands at the edge of the park and can be seen from as far away as 80kms. This cross commemorates a simple wooden cross placed here by De Maisonneuve, the founder of Montreal, *below* after Ville Marie was saved from a

giant flood in 1643. Travellers crossing Champlain Bridge *bottom left* still suffer during rush-hour but EXPO 67 brought the ultra modern Metro, a subway with silent rubber-tired trains and distinctively decorated stations *centre left*. Habitat at EXPO 67 is pictured *top left*.

1976 brought the Olympic Games to Montreal and, despite many problems, the Olympic Stadium was finished just in time.

No other city in the world is quite like Quebec City. Unique in every way, Quebec City is a natural citadel, marking the place where the St. Lawrence River first narrows (which is what 'Kebec' probably signified in the language of the Indians). Before the days of steam navigation, Quebec City was the key to the interior of the North American Continent. Hence, it served as the main-base for the great French explorers who probed as far west as the Rockies and south to the Gulf of Mexico; for above Quebec City, large sailing vessels dared not proceed. Quebec City is the capital of the Province of Quebec. It is principally a cultural and administrative centre with a good deal of light and some heavy industry. It is almost entirely French speaking and the quality of the Old World applies here more than in any other Canadian city.

A statue of Champlain *far left*, who founded Quebec City in 1608, overlooks the harbour and the lower town *overleaf*. An unmistakable landmark is, however, provided by the internationally famed hotel, the Château Frontenac *top left*, below which Dufferin Terrace provides a view onto Place Royale *top right* at the foot of Cap Diamant. For a number of years now the Quebec Government *above* has been conducting remarkable restoration work in this area of the lower town. In addition to the jewel that is Notre-Dame-des-Victoires church in Place Royale, one can visit vaulted cellars and opulent houses which belonged to merchants of the young colony.

Descending the Plains of Abraham, one is faced with some magnificent older houses on Avenue Saint-Denis *left* and Rue Saint-Louis *below* before returning again to Dufferin Terrace *centre left*. A ferry boat leaves the harbour for a brief trip to Levis *bottom left*.

The Laurentians, north of Quebec City is a region rich in distinctive characteristics. From the time of Champlain, the River Outaouais served as a main artery for the fur trade and later for the transportation of huge white pine logs needed by England during the Napoleonic wars. Today the Laurentians offer recreation not only to the residents of Montreal and Quebec City but also to visitors from other provinces and from the United States. Resort centres like Greyrocks Inn, for instance, pictured here *top right* offer the finest skiing facilities during the winter months while autumn colours *below right* fascinate artists and visitors from all over the world.

The jewel of the Gaspé peninsula is certainly Percé *far left and below*. It is one of the most remarkable natural wonders of the world. The village, set in fantastic surroundings, is 74 km. from Gaspé and bears the name of the world-famous rock which dominates the beach. Facing Percé is Bonaventure Island *above* which is a wild bird refuge. Thousands of gulls and gannets inhabit the island. Several times daily, during the summer, boats carry visitors on a tour of the island.

NEW BRUNSWICK

Fredericton *left* is New Brunswick's capital and a city of stately elms, historic buildings and reminders of its famous adopted son, Lord Beaverbrook, who came here as a child, studied law at University of New Brunswick and went into business. He accumulated a fortune, entered British politics and eventually became a newspaper tycoon.

Saint John *centre left* became rich and famous in the 19th century because of its timber industry and its ship-yards. Millville *bottom left* is only one of the many picturesque communities in New Brunswick.

The rocks at Hopewell Cape, near the mouth of the Petitcodiac River, were formed over many centuries by wind, frost and the sea. At high tide they look like tree-covered islands but low waters reveal more interesting shapes *above*.

Sunset over the Bay of Fundy *right*.

NOVA SCOTIA

Halifax (*below*, Cogswell Street and *bottom right*, Grand Parade),
Capital of Nova Scotia, is the biggest city of the Atlantic provinces.
The city is surrounded by water and its fine harbour with 32 berths
can accommodate even the largest vessels. Also on a peninsula,
Lunenburg *top left*, with its back and front harbours, is an ideal
location for fishing in the waters of the Banks, where the Labrador
current meets the Gulf Stream. About 42kms. from Halifax is Peggy's
Cove *below centre and top right*, favourite spot of artists and one of
Canada's most photographed places, famed for its trim houses,
weatherworn wharves and colourful fishing boats. Not only Peggy's
Cove, but many more little harbours such as Pent de Grat *far left, below*,
Indian Habour, *below left* and Springfield *bottom* along Nova
Scotia's lovely coastline invite the visitor to stay for a while.

PRINCE EDWARD ISLAND

Charlottetown is Canada's smallest provincial capital and the only city of Prince Edward Island. It is called, with affection, the birthplace of Canada, for here the Fathers of Confederation met for the first time in September 1864 (*centre left* the Province House). Prince Edward Island National Park

has some of the finest white sand beaches *above*, towered over by huge red sandstone cliffs as high as 30 metres. The park extends for about 40kms. along the north shore of the island. Here Lucy Maud Montgomery, immortalized this house near Cavendish *top left* in her book "Anne of Green Gables". Nearby North Rustico *bottom left*, a small fishing village, offers exhibits of animals native to the Maritime provinces in the Prince Edward Island Wildlife Park.

Profits Point Lighthouse is depicted *opposi*

In 1949, Newfoundland, once Britain's oldest colony, became Canada's tenth and youngest province. Below the majestic rock and the old guns of Signal Hill lies its capital, St. John's *above left*. Ships from many nations visit the port of St. John's, and the bars and shops along Water Street – the oldest street in North America – are alive with foreign languages. Not so foreign is the toast, as a Newfoundlander raises his glass of Screech, a strong West Indian Rum bottled in St. John's: "I looks towards ye", to which the response: "And I bows accordin'", is required.

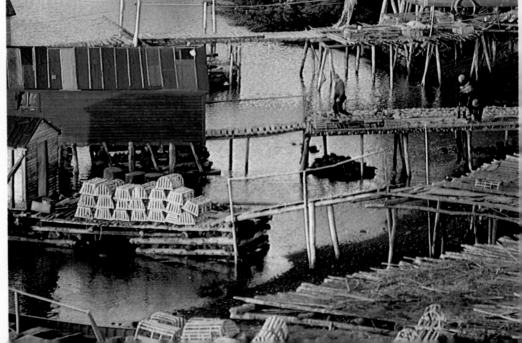

NEWFOUNDLAND

Top right Fogo Island.
Above Brigus on Conception Bay not far
from St. John's.
Far left Tizzards Harbour.
Left Fishing.

127

Published in 1981 by Colour Library International Ltd.
Photography © Colour Library International Ltd.
Separations by La Cromolito, Milan, Italy
Printed and bound by JISA-RIEUSSET, Barcelona, Spain
Display and text filmsetting by Focus Photoset, London
All rights reserved
I.S.B.N. 0-8317-8700-7
COLOUR LIBRARY INTERNATIONAL.